Time Management

A Guide To Efficiently Managing Time By Strategically Organising Your Daily And Weekly Schedules

(Enhancing Productivity Through The Utilisation Of Technology, Methodologies, And Strategic Approaches)

Patrick Nielsen

TABLE OF CONTENT

Enhanced Effectiveness And Output 1

Learn To Outsource And Delegate 11

Characteristics And Objectives Of A Superb Time Manager 17

Actions That Typically Lead To Insufficient Time Management. 66

On Time Every Time 87

Evaluating Your Abilities In Time Management 97

The Growth Of Work From Home 117

Collaboration And Communication That Works 130

Time Management 141

Tips For Cooking 162

Enhanced Effectiveness And Output

As was previously indicated, you will discover that your efficiency increases on its own as soon as you develop time management skills. You will be able to complete more work in a shorter amount of time when your efficiency rises. To put it another way, you become more productive as well. One major factor that contributes to our decreased efficiency is the speed at which we complete the tasks on our to-do list. Haste has an impact on our accuracy and, consequently, our productivity. In a similar vein, we simply cannot pull off this exhausting experience of running behind schedule. In due order, the effort will undoubtedly catch up and affect our productivity. Low levels of efficiency are also linked to low productivity. Therefore, we must have good time management skills.

✓ Personal Control

We develop a sense of discipline through time management. How many times have our friends treated us rudely because we consistently back out of social events? How many significant birthdays and anniversaries have we missed? Not to mention how many times we have failed to submit our applications by the deadline.

There are very few things that may go wrong when your day is planned out in detail. You get better at setting aside time for everything, including work, phone calls, and leisure pursuits. You ultimately have to teach your mind to function within the restrictions of your time. In this manner, you'll discover that you have adequate time for both work and play without letting anyone down. Aside from that, you'll come to understand that life is more than just work and begin to appreciate the significance of finding a balance between your professional and social lives.

These are a few of the key justifications for time management. All aspects of your life are connected to time management, which enables you to set aside time for each worthwhile work without skipping any.

TM Cutting Down on Clutter

In addition to bringing order into your life, efficient time management is a useful ability that will support you in achieving your long-term objectives. By assisting you in comprehending the motivations behind the daily chores you complete and encouraging you to take proactive steps toward completing the smaller tasks that lead to the larger goals you have set for yourself, this skill effectively gives your life meaning.

In actuality, certain chores are easier to endure or do when they have a reason.

For instance, cleaning is a chore that most people dislike, but it is necessary if the home is to be tidy and orderly. This makes cleaning a decision rather than a chore we feel obligated to complete.

Time management skills guarantee that the most important aspects of your life are given the most productive time, which will significantly increase your productivity overall. However, efficient time management will enable you to work less, not more, productively. Time is one of the most precious commodities you have, and once it's gone, it's never coming back. If you approach every activity as a top priority, you'll undoubtedly acquire negative time management habits that drain your energy without increasing your productivity. This practice of "making every task an emergency" is detrimental to both our time and our health.

✓ Monitor your advancement: Your responsibility doesn't stop with goal-setting. We won't be able to gauge the amount of time spent on it until we monitor our advancement toward reaching these objectives. Referring back to the earlier example, our objective is to run five laps at the neighbourhood park each day. I think you could finish the five laps in under thirty minutes. On the other side, you might find that it takes you longer than thirty minutes to do the laps if you run without a watch. This is the reason why having quantifiable objectives is crucial. However, setting measurable goals is pointless if you don't periodically monitor your progress.

Keeping a journal might be a useful tool for tracking your development. In this manner, you'll be able to evaluate your performance every day and spot any irregularities. Additionally, this will assist you in recognizing impractical objectives and guiding your decision-making process. Stated differently, systematically monitoring your advancement enables you to pinpoint any time wasters and provide solutions.

How to Deal with Having to Postpone Plans

Remind them of your importance to them and explain your cancellation.

Find out from them how they are doing.

Offer a different day and hour.

Finish with "I appreciate your understanding."

While some of these ideas may appear more appropriate in a professional context, you may modify and apply them in other contexts as well. Making the other person feel important and letting them know you cherish your time with them is crucial. In order to try to view them again, you also want to bring up a different day and time.

Though there's no assurance you'll be able to carry out all of your goals, at least you're trying. You are managing your time in multiple ways just by trying. By taking charge of your life, you are giving your priorities significance.

Although time is always passing, you don't have to rush it. If you plan, get organized, and let life happen, you can make a difference. Our lives are regularly disrupted by time, but it doesn't have to be. We don't have to put up with it anymore.

Make a change in your way of living and see how it transforms your entire existence.

In the upcoming chapter, we'll talk about how to bring about that long-lasting transformation and give ourselves a chance at success. We will discuss the many approaches to implementing and sustaining change.

Learn To Outsource And Delegate

You likely wear numerous hats during the day, regardless of your profession—whether you're a business owner, employee, or even a stay-at-home parent. Although this chapter will mostly address business owners, anyone can use the concepts.

People who are fed up with being employed frequently launch their own companies. They aspire to independence. But being an entrepreneur requires being more than just your boss. You are also your customer service department, your sales team, your secretary, your accountant, and your PR. The list goes on.

Not all of these duties are created equal, especially when taking your ROI (return on investment) into account.

Think for a moment about all of the various jobs you complete for your company in a given week. Put them in writing and review your business documentation later to determine how much time you're devoting to each of these activities.

Examining your company's bottom line is one of the finest methods to calculate your ROI. Think about how many hours you've put into a process like bookkeeping. Believe in how you make money. How much do you charge for your services, or if you sell goods, how much do you believe you can sell in the same amount of time?

If you charge $40 per hour for your services and spend ten hours a week on bookkeeping, for instance, you can end up spending $400 in a single week. That is not how you manage a business!

However, consider the human cost as well. What impact do the hours you spend working on your business have on your personal life, relationships with family and friends, and even your health? You could be spending those 40 hours a month on activities you enjoy with your friends and family instead of using them for JUST accounting procedures.

You don't actually have to do everything yourself, even if you do have your own company. Certain aspects of your business, and even your life, will ultimately suffer if you attempt. You cannot say to yourself, "Well, this is how they do it; I have to do it this way, too," by glancing at another person. Each person is unique, with varying abilities and comfort levels when it comes to certain duties. Learning how to manage your time and allocate time to your strengths is essential for productivity and success. If there are certain jobs that you are not excellent at, think about employing someone who is and assigning them to them.

Being able to assign and outsource work and recognize that others can complete necessary chores just as well—if not better—than you is a sign of effective time management. To free up more time for activities that will benefit you financially or that you like, take some time to calculate your ROI and discover how to assign duties that are using too much of your time.

Characteristics And Objectives Of A Superb Time Manager

It takes time to become a proficient time manager. It develops as you become more focused and disciplined. It occurs when you learn to categorize your short-term and long-term objectives. It occurs when you start to view time as something that can be controlled rather than as uncontrollable chaos. You will learn about the traits and objectives of a great time manager in this chapter.

In the last section of this chapter, which briefly discusses goal-setting, you will discover other ways to apply effectiveness and efficiency, urgency and importance. By the time this chapter ends, you ought to have a clear understanding of your traits and aspirations, as well as how to become a better time manager.

Mary prioritizes domestic chores and proofreading as her top two duties because she likes to finish the easy ones before moving on to the more challenging ones. She could only devote more time and energy to the third priority if the other, simpler jobs were finished first. In contrast, Mary felt that the task with the fourth priority needed more time and effort to complete and that its date was further away than any of her previous assignments. Observe how Mary kept the most challenging assignment for last when she could devote all of her time to her major goal and was relieved of all other obligations.

Setting priorities based on job value

The value of a particular activity or project is the focus of the third level of prioritization. Managers and businesswomen frequently employ this type of prioritization. Every work is evaluated for both its present worth and the potential revenue it can produce. Projects with high incomes or high values are ranked highest in the priority table, whereas projects with low incomes or low values are ranked below.

Take a look at the example priority table that contractor Mark made to manage his projects, their priorities, and their values.

Clients employ Mark to construct their ideal residences, workplaces, or public spaces. Due to Mark's established reputation in his field, his team has grown to handle multiple projects concurrently. Mark is aware that he needs to be specific about which tasks to take on first, though.

Project Value Closing Date First priority

1. Mr. and Mrs. Alison's condominium unit was roughly 1,500,000 $ in February 2016. Priority #3; 2. Mr. and Mrs. Garland's Retirement Home approximately 2,000,000 $ February 2016 Priority #2; 3. BASICS Pharmaceutical Branch approximately 3,000,000 $ March 2016 Priority #1

Take note of how Mark selected the condominium unit owned by Mr and Mrs Alison over the retirement home of Mr and Mrs Garland based on the project value. It may seem unjust to Mr. and Mrs. Alison, but in actuality, better-paid projects typically require more labour and time to finish. Therefore, Mark made the right choice in choosing the retirement home over the condominium. This clarifies why Mark gave the BASICS Pharmaceutical division the highest priority.

Establishment

A crucial component of efficient time management is time organization.

It might be difficult to prioritize projects, maintain attention, and finish work quickly if you are not organized.

Here are some time management strategies to help you reach your objectives and become more productive:

Establish a schedule: Scheduling is one of the best methods for managing your time. This is a schedule that lists your daily and weekly duties and activities. It can also be hourly in nature. You can prioritize work, manage your time more effectively, and maintain goal focus when you follow a timetable.

Establish objectives: You must give yourself clear, attainable objectives. This keeps you motivated and helps you concentrate on what matters. Make sure your objectives have a timeline, are quantifiable, and are achievable. Your goals can be divided into smaller chores, which you can then add to your timetable.

Make use of a task list: Having a task list helps you remain organized and guarantees that you don't overlook anything crucial. Ensure that your to-do list is up to date and accurately represents your current priorities.

Assign tasks: Assigning chores to others can free up your time so you can concentrate on more important work. Consider assigning less significant jobs that others can complete more quickly than you if you work in a team or with colleagues.

Reduce distractions as much as possible because they might squander important time and drastically lower productivity. Determine the typical sources of distraction and make every effort to minimize or remove them. This may include deleting pointless tabs on your computer, disabling your phone's notifications, or finding a quiet place to work.

Utilize time management tools: There are a number of tools available to assist you in maintaining organization and focus. You can use an app like a calendar to plan out your projects, a task manager to make and organize your to-do list, or a Pomodoro timer to focus for a set amount of time.

Make self-care a priority. Being well is crucial to being motivated and productive. This includes consuming a balanced diet, exercising frequently, and obtaining adequate sleep. It is important to schedule self-care activities and to give them the same priority as other tasks.

To sum up, time organization is essential to efficient time management. You may boost your productivity and accomplish your goals more quickly by making a timetable, setting objectives, using a task list, assigning duties, reducing distractions, utilizing time management apps, and placing self-care first.

To make sure your calendar still aligns with your current priorities and objectives, don't forget to check and tweak it frequently.

We'll talk about how to stop procrastinating and increase your efficiency in the next part.

Difficult Procrastination Mentality.....

Few behaviours in the complex web of human behaviour are as widespread as procrastination. Procrastination is a sophisticated dance of psychological intricacy, emotional conflict, and cognitive dissonance that is sometimes mistaken for a simple lack of discipline or a character flaw. In order to have a thorough understanding of the art of procrastination, we must first take a journey to comprehend the intricate reasoning behind this phenomenon. This chapter investigates the psychological framework where motivation and inertia meet, reveals the underlying dynamics that underlie our tendency to postpone and dives into the psychology of procrastinators.

Two Factors at Work

A delicate conflict between the long-term possibilities of fulfilment and the promise of instant gratification lies at the core of procrastination. One may argue that there is something almost mesmerizing about the allure of rapid satisfaction, whether it be through social media browsing, TV show bingeing, or indulging in a sweet snack. These pursuits offer instant gratification, stimulating the pleasure centres of our minds and offering a brief reprieve from responsibilities and stress. However, long-term goals need work, preparation, and a readiness to postpone satisfaction in order to reap greater rewards later on.

The dual aspect of the human psyche is closely linked to our evolutionary background. For our predecessors, finding quick access to resources like food, water, and shelter was crucial to their survival. Our biology is wired to prioritize the here and now above the future. But as society advances, so do the expectations made of us. Procrastination thrives in the friction that exists between our innate tendencies and our contemporary responsibilities.

The Illusion of Productivity

Paradoxically, productivity is sometimes sacrificed in favour of procrastination. When we put off doing essential chores, we tend to find solace in seemingly beneficial activities that don't really advance our long-term objectives. By deliberately delaying critical activities, we might deceive ourselves into thinking that we are actively working on them, a behaviour called "structured procrastination." For instance, we start to use our to-do lists, email, and workplace organization as stand-ins for the most difficult tasks we purposefully put off.

This false sensation of productivity acts as a buffer against the shame and worry that come with procrastinating, in addition to giving a momentary sense of accomplishment. We are able to momentarily escape the grip of self-doubt and the persistent sense of our impending responsibilities when we focus our efforts on side projects. The pleasure of these minor victories produces a deceptive impression of advancement that covers up the real issue, which is the avoidance of the really significant responsibilities.

The Perfectionism Paradox

Another scary psychological trait that frequently coexists with procrastination is perfectionism. Ironically, striving for perfection can cause stagnation and regression. Perfectionists frequently hold themselves to inflated expectations. Because of this, they become mired in a never-ending loop of self-doubt and worry that their output will never live up to the high expectations they set for themselves. They put off starting a task until the "perfect" circumstances arise because they are afraid of failing and want to avoid criticism or failure.

Perfectionism may be a drive as well as a hindrance. It pushes people to pursue greatness, but it can also instil a paralyzing fear of failing. The mentality of the procrastinator agrees that a task cannot be deemed a failure if it has not been started as a means of shielding itself from possible failure. Thus, perfectionism unintentionally fueled procrastination, trapping people in a never-ending cycle of delay.

The Function of Emotional Regulation

An important factor in the procrastinator's attitude is their emotions. When faced with jobs that make us feel bored, anxious, or uncertain, our natural tendency is to avoid them. Procrastination turns into a coping strategy that shields us from the unpleasantness of doing things that make us feel bad. While this kind of emotional avoidance can offer a brief respite, it also feeds back into the procrastination cycle and creates a negative feedback loop. Furthermore, the mood-altering properties of activities that provide instant rewards also serve to momentarily eliminate negative emotions. In the short term, comfort food and social media browsing can help reduce tension and anxiety. These hobbies, however, just serve as band-aid fixes and don't deal with the underlying issues that are causing our mental misery. We can start to develop more healthy techniques for emotional engagement and regulation by comprehending and identifying the emotional foundations of procrastination.

The Incapacity of Too Much

Our lives are so complicated these days that we are frequently faced with an excessive amount of work, choices, and obligations. Our capacity to act may be hampered by psychological paralysis brought on by this overwhelm. When presented with an overwhelming list of tasks, the brain's default setting is to become inactive. We may enter the well-known realm of procrastination due to our fear of failing or our conviction that we are incapable of handling such a heavy workload.

In addition, an era of perpetual connectedness and information overload has been brought about by the digital age. We become constantly distracted by the never-ending barrage of emails, messages, and attention requests. In this situation, procrastination turns into a coping strategy to deal with the deluge of obligations and information, in addition to a psychological reaction.

In brief

The intricate analysis of procrastination uncovers a complicated web of entwined, opposing influences that mould our actions. The psychological landscape of the procrastinator is a battlefield where archaic impulses collide with contemporary responsibilities, from the seductive temptation of rapid satisfaction to the imperceptible constraint of emotional avoidance. Even though it stems from a passion for excellence, the quest for perfection may unintentionally fuel obsolescence. The paralysis of overwhelm casts a shadow over our ability to act, and the illusion of work conceals the real avoidance of crucial duties.

As we continue to explore the fundamentals of procrastination, we must never forget that the first step toward emancipation is comprehending complex thinking. By breaking down psychological layers of complexity, we can better comprehend the causes of our regressive inclinations. Equipped with this understanding, we can start dissecting the art of procrastination and make proactive moves in the direction of change.

We will continue to examine the complex nature of procrastination in the upcoming chapters, as well as its causes, effects, and—above all—the tactics that help us break free from its hold. Let's embrace the complexity of our thoughts and work our way through the maze-like pathways that lead to long-lasting transformation as we set out on this quest for autonomy.

1. The Princes and the Seven Fishes

❖❖❖

Previously, there existed a monarch with seven sons. The seven princes went out on their seven horses one day. After engaging in some fishing, the princes took turns catching Fish, which they then spread out to dry on the ground. All but one of the Fish, though, dried. The seven princes began to worry now. They were curious as to why the one Fish failed to dry.

They thus questioned the Fish itself. Why didn't you dry off, Fish?"

"Dear princes, there is grass on the ground, so I could not dry," the Fish answered.

"Grass, why are you still on the ground?" the princes inquired."

"The cow did not eat me," the grass shot back.

Next, the princes approached the cow. "Why didn't you eat the grass, cow?"

"The farmer did not feed me the grass," the cow retorted.

The princes then questioned the farmer: "Farmer, why did you not feed the cow grass?"

"Because my mother did not feed me today," the farmer retorted.

"Mom, why did you not feed your son the farmer?" the princes subsequently proceeded to ask the farmer's mother."

"My baby was crying, so I didn't get to feed the farmer," the mother retorted.

The young infant was then questioned by the princes, "Why were you crying?"

"The ant bit me," the infant retorted.

When the princes discovered the ant, they questioned it, "Why did you bite the baby?"

In response, the ant said, "Will I not bite the baby if she sticks her finger in my house?"

When they realized the ant was right, the princes leapt with delight. They thus gathered their horses, rode back to their fort, and led contented lives. The story comes to an end there.

When I was a child, this was the first story I ever heard. This is still the first story that comes to me when I have to tell one to children. This short narrative initially seemed to have no morals. Although it appeared to have nothing to teach, as I told this story again and over, I realized there was something important to learn. It was this story that inspired me to begin writing this book. What lessons can be learned from this seemingly straightforward tale?

Lessons from Layman

a. Taking the necessary curiosity and delving deeply into the issue to find a solution

Investigating thoroughly is necessary to determine the root cause of the issue. Scanning the surface of the issue won't solve it; at best, it can only provide minimally temporary comfort. In this case, the princes could have ceased asking questions in the first or second phase, or they could have disregarded the fact that only one Fish failed to dry. Rather, they continued and weren't content until they discovered the true reason why the Fish wasn't drying. Their curiosity enabled them to identify a likely reason.

Throughout the procedure, they did not hold back or hesitate to question anyone—whether it was a kid, an animal, or even just grass. This demonstrates that, in terms of leadership abilities, a manager or supervisor shouldn't hesitate to question those at the bottom of the hierarchy about an issue. A boss ought to take into account all recommendations. Often, the most creative solutions to challenging puzzles come from the imaginations of novices or enthusiasts.

A shoe is lost for lack of nails, a horse is lost for lack of shoes, and a rider is lost for lack of horses.

The adage above, which I also recently read, appears to fit quite nicely with the present narrative. The narrative and the adage above emphasize how ignoring little warning indicators can have serious consequences. Their shadows were cast before them by the impending events. According to my experience, it's better to be extra cautious than careless.

b. Don't rely on assumptions; instead, explicitly address some of the issues.

Naturally, it's impossible to ask a dead fish why it didn't dry! Rather, I want to show that if someone is a part of the issue, then they are equally a part of the solution. Asking or confronting the person directly who is creating or causing the issue is preferable to using a backdoor or assuming a response before inquiring. Asking direct questions can simply and quickly resolve issues in both personal and professional relationships. Clear communication contributes to the prevention of misconceptions. In this tale, the princes questioned the Fish directly, asking, "What is the problem?" as their first action. Thus, instead of speculating and making assumptions on their own, they could at last identify the source.

Step Six:

The Strength of Stacking Habits

H

Bit stacking is an effective way to establish and maintain new habits. By connecting a new habit to an already-existing one, you can make it easier to incorporate into your daily routine. For instance, if you plan to get ready in the morning right after your typical morning routine, factor in an additional ten minutes.

Habit stacking is another option to overcome tardy tendencies. You may also set an alarm for 15 minutes earlier in the day to serve as a reminder to keep on schedule if you frequently find yourself running late in the afternoon. These prompts have the potential to be quite effective in both forming new habits and ending unhealthy ones.

You may also utilize habit stacking to establish daily routines that serve as a reminder of your priorities and ambitions. To help you stay on track throughout the day, consider creating a morning ritual that entails evaluating your daily agenda and making a goal. Similarly, making it a nightly practice to evaluate your day and record any lessons you learned is a fantastic method to hold yourself responsible.

Maintaining these routines on a regular basis can help you make better decisions and bring about long-lasting change. Thus, don't delay; begin habit stacking right now! When it comes to kicking bad tardiness habits and moving closer to your objectives, a little bit goes a long way.

Chapter 3: Organizing Your Environment for Better Time Management: From Chaos to Clarity

Trash is more than just tangible items. It's poor habits, poisonous connections, and outdated beliefs. Anything that doesn't help you be your best self is clutter. –Peter Walsh

As someone who enjoys gathering emotional objects and trinkets, I've come to understand that clutter may have a big negative effect on your productivity and mental health. Clutter can make your room feel overpowering and increase your stress and anxiety levels. It might be mentally draining to continually feel as though you have a ton of work to accomplish.

Clutter has an impact not only on your emotional state but also on your ability to concentrate on things. It might be challenging to focus on just one thing at a time when your surroundings are congested because you could be quickly distracted by the things around you. It might be challenging to focus when it feels like your attention is being drawn to a lot of different places all the time.

Let's be honest. Stacks of paper, mountains of clothes, and a workstation hidden beneath a layer of mess—we've all been there. Even figuring out where to begin might be daunting. An untidy workspace can be detrimental to your mental health and creative flow. Your mind is prone to overloading when you are in a hectic environment. It's difficult to think creatively or unconventionally in a disorderly and chaotic setting. When your workspace is tidy and well-organized, you might discover that you're more inspired and creative.

Negative emotions like guilt, humiliation, and frustration can also be triggered by disorder. You can frequently feel angry and guilty for not being able to keep your area tidy and for not being able to locate the things you require. You may eventually come to understand that creating routines and habits to maintain order in your surroundings can help counteract these negative consequences.

We'll take you on a tour of the fascinating realm of organization in this chapter. We'll help you turn your disorganized and disorderly surroundings into a calm and useful area. We'll investigate the intriguing relationship between your surroundings and your capacity for sustained concentration and productivity.

We'll go over everything from organizing your physical area to setting up efficient work management tools and reducing outside distractions so you can stay focused. But we won't just hand you a bunch of theoretical guidelines and disappear, leaving you on your own. We'll provide you with doable, simple-to-apply techniques to help you clear your area, reduce outside distractions, and take charge of your time and surroundings.

You will have the information and resources necessary to establish an atmosphere that encourages you to reach your objectives and keeps you on track at the end of this chapter. You'll experience firsthand how a little structure can significantly increase your productivity and general well-being, and you'll feel empowered to take on any problem.

Workplace Marvels

Assume you are now seated at your workstation. Take a moment to scan your surroundings and evaluate the state of affairs. Is chaos all around you?

Is there enough light? How is your desk arranged to maximize productivity?

The first step in setting up your workstation for the best possible time management is to evaluate what you currently have there. While this may seem difficult, it is important to determine what is functioning properly and what requires improvement. Take a few deep breaths and settle into a calm frame of mind to begin. After that, take a tour of your office and consider it from various perspectives. Examine your chair, workstation, lighting, and other room furnishings.

As you evaluate your surroundings, think about these inquiries:

● How disorganized is my work area? Are there heaps of books, papers, or other stuff that need to be disposed of?

● Does the setup of my desk encourage productivity? Are the things I frequently use readily available? Do I have a system in place to keep papers and other materials organized?

● Does the room have enough lighting? Do I need to strain my eyes to see everything I need to see?

● Do I need to remove any distractions from my workspace?

● Is my chair supportive and comfy? Is my posture while sitting promoting proper alignment and avoiding strain on my neck and back?

These are not judgmental questions; rather, they are meant to assist you in evaluating your degree of organization and clutter without fear of embarrassment or condemnation. When responding to these inquiries, it's critical to be truthful and avoid using disarray or shoddy planning as an excuse. After you've evaluated your present surroundings, make a list of what needs to be improved. Set these things in order of urgency and begin implementing improvements. To increase productivity, think about organizing your workspace, getting a comfy chair, or clearing out clutter from your desk. By admitting the areas in which you need to improve, you may commit to changing for the better and raising your standard of living overall.

Reduce distractions by shutting off unused tabs and turning off alerts.

Distractions are easily accessible in our highly connected society with only a click or swipe. Our productivity and focus can be undermined by notifications from multiple apps, social media, and pointless browser tabs that constantly fight for our attention. It's critical to intentionally reduce these distractions in order to foster an environment that supports attentive work.

One of the most frequent causes of distraction on our gadgets is notifications, those tiny pings, vibrations, or banners. They are meant to capture our attention, and they do so well, frequently at the expense of our concentration and output. Studies have indicated that after a single interruption, it can take up to 23 minutes to fully resume focus. As a result, controlling these digital disruptions is essential to preserving productivity.

Turning off notifications when you need to focus is the easiest and most efficient approach to managing them. You may disable notifications on most devices and programs completely or selectively. For instance, you can turn off all notifications on your computer or smartphone for a predetermined amount of time by using the "Focus Mode" or "Do Not Disturb" settings. As an alternative, you can disable or alter the notifications in the settings of individual apps to suit your tastes.

Since email notifications frequently cause disruptions at work, they merit special attention. Instead of receiving emails automatically, think about disabling them and scheduling particular times each day to check your mailbox. This method, which is also known as "time batching," can assist you in more effectively managing your emails and preventing continual distraction.

The multitude of open tabs on our web browsers is another common source of distraction on our gadgets, even if turning off notifications can greatly reduce digital distractions. Keeping a lot of tabs open might cause your computer to run much slower, in addition to cluttering your digital workspace. Additionally, every open tab could be a distraction, taking your focus away from the work at hand.

To properly manage tabs in your browser, take into account these strategies:

1. Conscious Tab Management: Pay attention to the tabs you are now using. As soon as you are through with a tab, close it. This technique lessens the urge to switch jobs in addition to clearing clutter.

2. These include tab organizer extensions that can organize tabs by topic or shut down unused tabs automatically after a predetermined amount of time, as well as tab suspender extensions that put idle tabs to sleep to conserve resources.

3. Single-Tab Working: Make it a challenge to just use one tab at a time. By removing the chance of tab-based distractions, this technique can

significantly improve your focus and productivity.

4. Bookmarking and Read-It-Later Services: Take into consideration bookmarking or using a read-it-later service like Pocket if you come across intriguing articles or resources that you wish to read but aren't immediately relevant. In this manner, when you have time to access the material later, you can close the tab and still have access to it.

Even though these techniques can be quite helpful in lowering digital distractions, it's also critical to have a physical workspace that encourages concentrated concentration. This could entail hiding your phone from view, employing noise-cancelling headphones, or organizing your workspace.

To sum up, controlling browser tabs and notifications can help minimize distractions and provide a more focused and effective work environment. It's a proactive strategy that calls for discipline and constant work. Recall that every notification that is turned off or pointless tab that is closed is a step toward a more concentrated and effective work session. Ultimately, these minor actions can result in considerable enhancements to your output and overall work-life equilibrium.

Actions That Typically Lead To Insufficient Time Management.

Many of us are aware that we could be using our time more wisely, but it can be challenging to identify the things we are doing poorly and to understand how we could do better. However, when we execute time management well, we become extremely productive at work and experience a significant reduction in stress. We may dedicate time to engaging, high-payoff projects that have the potential to significantly impact a career.

Ineffective time management causes employees to miss deadlines, produce mediocre work, become too anxious and upset, and run out of time. Ineffective time management has a negative effect on staff, management, and the company.

We'll examine some of your habits that often lead to poor time management in this section.

● Not keeping track of your to-do list

Have you ever had the persistent feeling that you should have completed a crucial task? If so, you most likely don't use a to-do list as a means of staying organized. (Or, if you do, you might not be making the most of it!)

Setting priorities for the tasks on your list is the difficult part of making effective use of to-do lists. A – F coding scheme is employed by many people, where A represents high-priority themes, and F represents extremely low priorities (A for high-priority things, F for very low priorities). Alternatively, you might use digits like A through D to simplify things.

If you're not careful, the entries for large jobs on your list may be ambiguous and ineffective. Say, for example, that you wrote, "Start on the budget proposal." But what exactly does this mean? This lack of information may cause you to put off or forget important chores. As a result, be cautious to break down large tasks or projects into specific, doable steps so that nothing important is overlooked.

● Failure to Set Personal Goals

In six months, where would you like to be? How about at this time next year or in ten years? If not, it's time to set some goals for yourself!

Establishing personal goals is essential to time management success because they provide you with direction and a goal to work toward. Setting goals also enables you to distinguish between activities that are merely entertaining and those that are worthwhile.

● Not Setting Goals

While you're coming up with ideas for a new client, your assistant has just come in with a problem that they need you to handle immediately. You're sure you've almost thought of a brilliant idea for their marketing campaign, but this "emergency" might force you to lose your train of thought.

Setting priorities can be challenging at times, especially when there is a flurry of tasks that seem urgent. But, if you want to improve your time management, you must know how to set priorities for your tasks.

The Action Priority Matrix is one tool that can help you efficiently prioritize tasks. It can help you determine if a task is low-value "fill-in" work or high-yield and high-priority labour. If you understand the difference, you'll manage your time far more effectively throughout the day.

● Not Managing Distractions

Are you aware that for some of us, interruptions might cost us up to two hours a day? Just think of all the things you could accomplish if you had that time back!

Effewe'rely managing interruptions and avoiding distractions is essential if you want to take charge of your day and do your best work. For example, when you need to focus, stop talking on instant messaging and tell people when they're bothering you too much. Additionally, you ought to learn how to pay more attention, particularly in situations where there are lots of distractions.

● Delaying

Delaying tasks that you ought to be doing immediately is called procrastination. When you put off doing an assignment, you end up detesting it, feeling bad that you haven't started, and eventually, everything catches up with you when you don't finish it in time.

As an example, a useful strategy is to teach yourself that you will only be working on a task for ten minutes at a time don't. Procrastinators often feel overwhelmed and uneasy because they hold high expectations that they must complete a task from beginning to end. Rather, focus on making a quick initial investment of time. That's it!

Action Plans are another helpful tool that you could uncover. They let you break large projects into smaller, more manageable tasks so that you may complete little amounts at a time and easily see what needs to be done overall. By doing this, you may be able to prevent yourself from feeling overpowered while starting a new project.

TM Taking on Overly

Does it become difficult for you to say "no" to people? If so, you definitely have far too many projects and obligations on your schedule. Stress, low morale, and inferior perform "an" e could result from this.

Alternatively, you could be a micromanager, a person who demands to oversee or handle every aspect of the work themselves because they don't think anyone else can do it correctly. (This might not only affect managers; it could affect everyone!)

In any case, taking on too much work is a waste of time and could lead to you being known for your hasty, subpar work.

Learn the delicate art of saying "yes" to the person but "no" to the task in order to put an end to this. This skill lets you make an impression on the group while also al "owi" g you to establish "your" self. If the other person starts putting pressure on you to grant their request, practice quick thinking and remaining composed.

● Living Up to "Busy"

Being busy gives some people a rush. The barely met deadlines, the constant emails, the piles of papers piling up on the desk that "need" to be addressed, the rushed run to the meeting... What a burst of adrenaline!

The problem is that having an "addiction to activity" rarely means you're productive and might even be stressful.

Rather, make an effort to slow down and improve your t" me management skills."

● Handling tasks at once

Sandra frequently composes emails while speaking with clients on the phone in order to stay organized. Sandra believes that multitasking is a wise use of her time, but in reality, it can take her 20-40% longer to finish a list of tasks than if she completed the same list of tasks sequentially. She performs both tasks poorly as a result, which annoys her clients and results in her emails being riddled with mistakes.

Therefore, it is advisable to focus on one work at a time and to forget about multitasking. In this manner, you'll produce work of a higher calibre.

● Not Taking Rest Periods

It's a good idea to think that you can work for eight or ten hours, especially if you have a deadline to meet. However, it's difficult for anyone to focus and produce very high-quality work without giving their brains a break and a chance to recover.

Therefoit'sdon't consider breaks to be "wasting time." They provide much-needed downtime, which stimulates creative thinking and facilitates productivity.

If you find it difficult to stop "working, schedule breaks for yourself or use an alarm clock to serve as a reminder. Take a quick walk, have a coffee, or just sit at your desk and practice meditation. Every hour or two, try to take a five-minute break. Additionally, remember to give yourself enough time for lunch because you won't be able to produce your best work while you're hungry!

● Inefficient Task Scheduling

Do you prefer the mornings? Or do you find that won't the sunset in the evening, your energy will increase you're? Each of us has unique rhythms or specific times of the day when we are most alert and productive.

The significance of effectively managing your time

The ability to give time purpose and enable people to maximize their time is what makes time management relevant. It is used in a corporate setting to specify goals and standards for groups and their employees. Good time management abilities enable people to achieve their goals and produce top-notch work. Additionally, time management enables managers to set realistic goals and recognize the capabilities of their workforce.

Making thoughtful decisions about what one wants to do is part of time management. People who are not good at managing their time react to outside stimuli all the time and become less in control of their lives and careers.

Not Being Aware of Your Own Time

Without a doubt, the most valuable resource in anyone's life is time. Everybody has access to the whole 365 days a year, seven days a week, and twenty-four hours a day. Though everyone has the same amount of time, why do some people manage to accomplish so much more than others? The explanation is simple: because they are conscious of how they spend their time, they are just better at managing it. They eliminate all of the pointless distractions.

Suppose you lament the lack of time in your life. It merely indicates that you are unaware of the passing of time.

I'll offer you a list of the things that people do that they don't even realize are a waste of time. Everyone should review this list in order to realize that perhaps some of the things aren't just habits but are meaningful pursuits that enhance life satisfaction.

Let's start with the most important one: media consumption. Now is the moment for you to be really honest with yourself. When you reflect on your day, ask yourself if it aligns with your goals and where your time has gone.

Suppose we examine a few of the most current figures. This is how it seems. A typical person works eight to nine hours a day, sleeps seven to eight hours, and watches media for roughly five hours a day.

This is astounding—5 hours a day is not insignificant at all. During this period, you could have achieved your goals, which could include finishing a project, starting a business, or just spending more time with your loved ones. I've been with a lot of folks, and they'vethey'vemented their lack time. However, when I probed further about their daily activities, I consistently found that they did not have time; they were just unaware that they were wasting it on media consumption.

Does this imply that you shouldn't play video games or watch movies? No, you just need to maintain balance. Let's talk about the fix. The first step to finding a relationship should be to be conscious of how much time you spend consuming media. Sincerity: Let's Pause and ask yourself if your actions are consistent with the life you wish to lead. If not, you should cut back on the amount of media you watch. Take action that will advance your career or quality of life. Consider listening to an audiobook or podcast about business, creativity, personal growth, etc., instead of watching a pointless YouTube video.

Of course, media is not the only thing where you waste your time, but undoubtedly, it's the major one. Other things many people spend their precious time on are texting and messaging. Messaging and texting spend an enormous amount of time. The most harmful part about messaging is that you can't take the time it takes because normally, people message in between their work; for every single text, they spend 20-30 seconds and can't access 30 seconds each time; you lose a significant amount of time without even letting you know.

The only solution to fix this is to dedicate a certain and definite period to respond to all the messages you have received.

Anyhow, if the messages are too urgent to react, you have to text them, but immediately after answering the texts, put your phone at a minimum distance of 5-10 feet from you, which will create a little resistance between you and your cellphones.

When I meet people around me, I often find a common problem: Everyone has at least one friend in their life with whom they don't want to spend time, but they still do it every day. I believe you should spend time with friends and family members who understand who you understand and who are actually there for you and vice versa.

In the end, it isn't aisn'tthe number of your friends but the meaningful, quality ones.

isn't

isn't

On Time Every Time

Punctuality is crucial in life. It shows that you respect other people's time and attention, and it can have an impact on your career. But what does being punctual mean? Why is it helpful? What are some ways to be more punctual? Let's find out!

It is important to be punctual. Punctuality is the trait of being able to finish a specified work or fulfil an obligation before or at a previously designated time. This can be an important trait in many different areas, including school and work.

Although there are many benefits to being on time, being late is considered rude because it shows that you do not respect other people's time. In addition, if you are late for work or school, it will affect everyone else in your class and make them have to wait for you to arrive, which could cause problems for both parties involved.

Punctuality benefits your family, friends, and community. Punctuality can be learned.

There is a right way and a wrong way to do things. When you arrive late, it's like you're saying that your family and friends don't matter enough for you to show up on time. If you have plans with someone, be sure that the other person understands what time it is and when the meeting will take place. This will give them plenty of time to get ready for their date or event without having to rush around at the last minute.

If an event starts at 8 p.m., be there before 7:50 p.m. If an event starts at 6 p.m., try arriving by 5:45 p. There should never be any doubt in anyone's mind as to whether or not someone will show up on time because they've already told that person what their expectations are when it comes down to punctuality.

Punctuality is good.

It's good for the person who comes on time because they get to do what they need to do without wasting any time. It's also good for everyone else involved. When someone shows up late, it throws off their schedule and affects other people in meetings or appointments or whatever else is happening at that moment.

When you're running late, try telling yourself that punctuality matters—especially because plenty of people are counting on you! The next time you're rushing around trying to leave work early, remind yourself that if you arrive ten minutes later than planned (or earlier), no one will thank you for your delay; instead, they'll be annoyed by it—and rightly so!

Punctuality is important because it shows respect and consideration for others.

- IT'S JUST NICE TO SHOW UP ON TIME.
- YOU'RE A DECENT HUMAN BEING, AND YOU DON'T WANT TO MAKE OTHER PEOPLE WAIT FOR NO REASON. IF YOU'RE GOING TO BE LATE, LET THEM KNOW WHY AND WHEN THEY CAN EXPECT YOU.

- YOU'LL BE MORE PRODUCTIVE IF THE OTHERS IN YOUR GROUP START ON TIME—YOU WON'T HAVE TO MAKE UP FOR LOST TIME LATER ON IN THE PROJECT.

Learning to be on time takes a conscious effort, especially if you've always been late.

- IT TAKES PRACTICE TO BE ON TIME
- YOU NEED TO CREATE A HABIT OF BEING ON TIME AND THEN STICK WITH IT.
- MAKE SURE YOU'RE NOT RUSHING THROUGH YOUR MORNING ROUTINE BECAUSE YOU'RE RUNNING LATE.

Start small. If you're almost never on time, don't make "being on time" your goal. You're more likely to be successful that way.

If you're someone who isn't usually punctual, it's probably not realistic to expect yourself to be on time every time. Instead of making that your goal, start small. For example, if you have an appointment at the DMV and tend to arrive late, set a goal for yourself to get there ten minutes earlier than usual. Once you've accomplished this goal a few times in a row, try aiming for fifteen minutes early instead!

When we set really high goals for ourselves (like "I will be on time for every single event I attend from now on"), it can sometimes lead us to feel discouraged when we don't meet those standards. But suppose we break down our goals into smaller parts and start with the ones that seem more manageable (like showing up ten minutes earlier than usual). In that case, we can build up those positive feelings until they become automatic responses.

Make sure you know where you're going or how to get there before you leave the house.

Before you leave the house, take a look at your itinerary. If you're not sure about how to get there or where to go once you arrive, this can be a cause of punctuality problems. The best way to avoid this is by planning and making yourself familiar with the route beforehand; if that's not possible, bring along directions and ask someone familiar with the area for help on your way over.

Be respectful of other people's time, especially if they've kept an appointment open just for you.

● be respectful of other people's time, especially if they've kept an appointment open just for you.

● if you're late to get somewhere, let the people there know that you're running behind. they may not be able to wait around forever, and it will help them if they know how much longer they'll have to wait on you.

● try not to make yourself too important by keeping other people waiting for no reason at all.

always be kind when addressing lateness with others, and be willing to listen to their side of the story.

- always be kind when addressing lateness with others, and be willing to listen to their side of the story.

- if someone is consistently late, then there may be an underlying problem that needs attention. it could be a personal issue (for example, chronic lateness could indicate depression or anxiety), or it could be a professional one (for example, working in a job where deadlines are not flexible). you can help your co-worker by talking about what might cause the lateness and ways to handle it.

Evaluating Your Abilities In Time Management

An essential professional skill to have is the ability to manage your time well. By organizing your daily chores, you can prioritize projects, finish work on time, and keep bosses and coworkers informed of your progress. You can advance your profession and achieve important goals by practising efficient time management.

In this tutorial, we'll examine nine essential time management skills and how to hone and showcase them while looking for work.

If you are competent at managing your time, you can manage your time more effectively. Among the most important abilities in time management are:

1. Planning

If you maintain organization, you could be able to recall what has to be done and when. Being well-organized includes:

Keeping a current calendar.

Having easy access to particular documents.

Keeping your surroundings clean.

Taking precise, in-depth notes.

Scheduling important files in an organized manner speeds up the process of recovering them and reduces time wasted on pointless searches. Important documents should be stapled together.

• Don't leave piles of paperwork or folders piled high on your desk. Get rid of everything you don't need.

• Store personal items like your wallet, car keys, and cell phone in their designated places, together with stationery.

• Develop the habit of using an organizer. Arrange your schedule in advance.

- Avoid writing on discarded paper. Always carry a pen and paper with you.

2. Setting priorities

If you want to manage your time effectively, you must prioritize each of your obligations. There are numerous methods for prioritizing jobs based on their importance. You may choose to start with shorter, easier duties and work your way up to longer, more difficult ones. Alternatively, you might prioritize your duties, beginning with the most pressing, or you could mix the two.

Rank the order of your tasks.

- Decide what your main priorities are. One shouldn't work just for the sake of working.

- Make a "Task Plan" or "To Do" list. Note the time that you start working. List all the things you need to get done in a day and rank them in order of priority and urgency.

- Urgent chores ought to be completed as soon as possible. Start your day by taking care of anything that doesn't need your immediate attention.

- Check off the things you've finished. • Workers must be able to distinguish between high- and low-priority jobs, as well as between vital and urgent work. It provides you with a sense of comfort and purpose.

• Steer clear of useless activities. You will be indolent and squander the whole day.

· Understand the duties and obligations of your position.

3. Establishing objectives

The first step to becoming a proficient time manager is setting goals. By creating objectives, you may quickly understand your final purpose and the priorities you need to establish. Having both short- and long-term goals will help you achieve success in the workplace.

4. Interaction

Gaining effective communication skills will enable you to convey your objectives and ideas to managers and fellow employees. In order to keep everyone on task, it can also help you ask timely questions and address concerns.

5. Organizing

Time management is an art form that demands preparation. By effectively organizing your day, meetings, and tasks, you can stay on schedule.

6. Assigning

You can practice assigning assignments if you are in charge of a project, even though supervisors are more likely to do so. It may be difficult to say "no" when someone asks you to do something at work, but setting boundaries is necessary if you want to manage your time well and eventually accomplish your goals.

7. Stress reduction

As you employ suitable time management strategies, keep your mental well-being in mind. Constructively managing your stress may help you stay motivated and work efficiently all day. This can be accomplished by rewarding yourself modestly when you complete chores or by taking short breaks during the day.

8. Solving issues

Proficient problem-solving skills will help you get over roadblocks and finish projects on schedule. Solving problems together will also help team members communicate with each other.

9. Making notes

Taking notes and keeping paperwork current is essential for time management and task completion. For example, you can waste time or have to redo some tasks if you follow outdated instructions.

Time management and mindfulness: Make mindfulness exercises a regular part of your day. By keeping you completely present and involved in every work, mindfulness can increase productivity and lower stress.

Time Management Apps: Make use of time management programs and applications that include functions such as goal-setting, task tracking, and time analysis. RescueTime, Asana, Trello, and Todoist are a few well-known programs.

Steer clear of perfectionism: A task may take longer than necessary to complete if you strive for perfection. It is sometimes the case that adequate is adequate. Develop the ability to assess when a task is adequately finished.

Effective Time Management in Meetings: By creating clear agendas, assigning precise time restrictions for each agenda item, and making sure that only pertinent individuals attend, you can keep meetings on track and productive.

Make Good Use of Waiting Time Take advantage of the times when you have to wait, like inline or when commuting. You can read articles, listen to instructional podcasts, or generate ideas.

Accept the Two-Do List: Keep a "to-don't" list in addition to your "to-do" list. This is a list of things you purposefully avoid doing in order to maintain concentration on your top goals.

Batching Email Responses: Set aside particular periods of the day to review and answer emails, as opposed to replying to them as they come in. This stops emails from being interrupted constantly.

Regularly Clear Your Workspace: Distraction and inefficiency can result from a messy workspace. Set aside a little period every day or every week to clean and arrange your workspace.

Employ Time Management Strategies: Try out several time management strategies, such as the Time Blocking Method, Getting Things Done (GTD), and the Pomodoro Technique. Select the one that best fits your working style.

Continuous Evaluation: Evaluate your time management efforts on a regular basis. Are you reaching your objectives on a regular basis? Do you need to stop engaging in any time-wasting behaviours that keep happening?

Give Authority Rather Than Just Tasks: Assign duties and decision-making authority when necessary. This lessens the need for continual supervision and gives others more authority.

Effective time management requires both a healthy body and mind that have had enough sleep.

Recognize How to Handle Distractions: Create coping mechanisms for when family members, coworkers, or phone calls interrupt. When necessary, express your demand for dedicated work time.

Illustration: Before you begin, visualize your day or your tasks. This kind of mental preparation might assist you in approaching your work with purpose and clarity.

Adapt and Evolve: Be prepared to modify your time management techniques as your obligations and environment do. The secret to long-term success is flexibility.

Page Four

Time tracking: To keep an eye on how you spend your time, use time-tracking software or apps. You may use this information to see trends, manage your time more wisely, and decide on your daily schedule with confidence.

The Zeigarnik Effect: According to this psychological theory, incomplete tasks frequently take up brain space and attention. To cut down on mental clutter, finish what you start or devise a clear plan for finishing it later.

Task Requirements: Determine which tasks require other tasks to complete. Set aside work that must be completed before moving on to more crucial tasks in order to maintain a productive workflow.

Parkinson's Law: As was previously indicated, responsibilities often grow to occupy the available time. Take advantage of this by establishing more focused, shorter deadlines to boost your output.

Time Management for Creativity: If you work on creative projects, set aside specific time slots during which you can be most creative. This is often in the morning for a lot of folks.

The 2-Hour Rule states that you should set aside at least two hours every day to work on your most important task without interruption. Over time, this persistent work might produce noteworthy outcomes.

The Ivy Lee Approach: List the six most crucial things you need to get done the following day after you finish each day. Give these chores top priority, and concentrate on finishing them before moving on to other things.

The 80/20 Rule (Pareto Principle) states that you should concentrate on the tasks and activities that have the biggest impact on your objectives. Usually, 20% of your work will result in 80% of your desired outcomes.

Task Juggling vs. Task Switching: Although it's typically not recommended to multitask, task juggling can work well for some tasks. This entails juggling several jobs that call for distinct kinds of concentration, like brainstorming and writing in succession.

Time Management and Decision Fatigue: Recognize that excessive decision-making might result in fatigue. To save mental strain, automate recurring decisions, establish routines, and simplify choices.

Effective time management techniques should be encouraged among team members if you are the team leader. Establish expectations, promote open communication, and give tools for teamwork.

The Email Management Four D's:

Apply the "Four D's" while handling emails: delete (unimportant emails).

Delegate (if you can).

Do (rapid replies).

Defer (plan a specified time to address).

Weekly Reviews: Evaluate your progress, modify your objectives, and make plans for the following week by doing weekly reviews. This supports your continued proactive time management strategy.

Time management and Goal Alignment: Make sure that the things you do on a daily basis support your long-term objectives. If a task doesn't help you achieve your goals, reevaluate its importance.

Appreciate Little Wins: As you progress toward your bigger objectives, note and celebrate your little victories. You can stay on track and become more motivated with this encouraging feedback.

The Growth Of Work From Home

The nature of employment has changed dramatically in recent years, impacting both how individuals make a living and how businesses run. This shift, which is sometimes called the "Rise of Remote Work," has upended preconceived ideas about the workplace, redesigned job structures, and questioned accepted practices. What was once a fad has evolved into a fundamental change in the way we approach our jobs and work. We shall examine the main causes, advantages, difficulties, and long-term effects of remote labour on people and society in this essay.

The remote work revolution has been further spurred by firms' need to decrease overhead costs, tap into global talent pools, and respond to changing market dynamics.

Flexibility in Remote Work Benefits: Unmatched flexibility is provided by remote work, which lets people choose their own workspaces and working hours. This flexibility facilitates employees' ability to manage work and personal obligations by promoting work-life balance.

Getting into a Worldwide Workforce: Global talent pools are available for organizations to draw from, offering a variety of viewpoints, expertise, and experiences.

Savings on costs: Remote employment has the potential to save large costs for both companies and workers. Businesses can cut costs on office space, and employees can save on daily meals, work clothes, and transportation.

Enhanced Output: Reduced Commute Stress: Reducing daily commute stress can improve mental and physical wellbeing. Some people believe that working remotely increases productivity since it allows them to personalize their work settings and reduces distractions.

Obstacles and Things to Think About

While there are many advantages to working remotely, there are drawbacks as well:

Isolation: Because remote workers miss out on the social contacts that take place in a regular office setting, working remotely can cause feelings of loneliness and isolation.

Communication Difficulties: In distant work environments, effective communication can be more difficult to achieve and calls for the use of digital tools and the development of strong online communication skills.

Work-Life Distinctions: Setting up boundaries is crucial since working remotely can make it difficult to distinguish between business and personal life.

Security and privacy: Strong cybersecurity measures are required in remote work situations since protecting sensitive data and preserving privacy might be more difficult.

The Enduring Effect

The advent of remote work is more than just a fad; it signifies a big change in the way we think about our jobs. Numerous experts believe that hybrid and remote work arrangements will persist. This change has important ramifications for many facets of society, including:

Real estate: As businesses downsize their physical footprints or repurpose office space for collaboration, the demand for office space may fluctuate.

Metropolitan Planning: As distant workers go outside of metropolitan centres for more reasonably priced and roomy housing arrangements, cities may see changes in the distribution of their population.

Transportation: Less commuting may result in fewer traffic jams and a reordering of transportation priorities.

Wellbeing and Mental Health: Both employers and employees are realizing the value of mental health care and wellbeing methods in remote work settings.

The emergence of remote work is changing how we live, work, and engage with the outside world. It presents opportunities and flexibility never before seen, but it also presents obstacles that call for creativity and adaptation. We must negotiate this shift by recognizing the advantages, resolving the difficulties, and maintaining our flexibility in the face of the constantly changing nature of work.

Utilizing the Trust Dimensions in a Workplace

Managing people, not only tasks, is your main duty as a manager. It is crucial to realize that your staff members are more than just resources that should be used on various tasks. They are aspirational, goal-oriented, emotional human beings. Being a good leader means showing people that you actually care about their welfare, both at work and outside of it.

Holding one-on-one meetings with your staff on a regular basis is one approach to show that you care. These discussions ought to cover more than just work-related topics. Talks about their personal life, aspirations, and professional objectives should also be included. Spend time getting to know them, asking open-ended questions, and demonstrating your sincere interest in their life.

By demonstrating an interest in your colleagues' personal lives, you may foster a more relaxed and transparent work environment that increases employee trust and loyalty. This can also assist you in determining areas in which they might require more resources or assistance, such as flexible work schedules or mental health services.

Talking with your staff about their career aspirations also shows them that you care about their growth and future. In addition to inspiring them to give their best work, this can assist you in identifying possible areas for internal growth or career advancement.

ACT NOW: Plan on checking in with your direct reports on a regular basis. Make a Google Doc for running notes that you can both add agenda items to.

Your team needs to normalize providing and accepting feedback. You must regularly and in a variety of ways ask your employees for input if you want to achieve this.

The Value of Effective Time Management

Everyone should work to acquire the important skill of time management. To maximize productivity and accomplish your goals quickly entails organizing and arranging how you spend your time. It is impossible to exaggerate the significance of time management because it affects both our personal and professional lives.

Making the most of the little time we have each day is one of the main advantages of good time management. Consequently, this enables us to be more productive overall and do more tasks in less time.

Reducing stress levels is another benefit of effective time management. We may prevent ourselves from becoming worried or overwhelmed by an excessive workload when we have a clear strategy for how we will spend our time. Alternatively, we can approach every assignment with motivation and focus, knowing that we can finish it on schedule.

Effective time management not only lowers stress but also enhances general health and wellbeing. We have more time when we efficiently manage our time to spend with our loved ones, take care of ourselves, and participate in enjoyable activities. Our general quality of life, as well as our bodily and mental health, may benefit from this.

On the other hand, ineffective time management can seriously harm our lives.

To sum up, time management is an essential skill that everyone ought to work to acquire. Effective time management allows us to increase output, lower stress levels, and enhance our general quality of life.

Collaboration And Communication That Works

Effective Gatherings

Though they are an essential component of working life, meetings can be a major time waster if they are not conducted well. To maximize the time in your meeting, make sure to ↬ Clearly state the goal and agenda.

☞ Only invite those who are truly necessary.

☞ Establish a rigorous deadline and follow it.

Encourage involvement and steer the conversation in the right direction.

You can cooperate effectively, exchange information, and make decisions in ineffective meetings.

Email Handling

Sending emails can quickly turn into a laborious chore. Effectively manage your inbox by setting aside specified times to read and reply to emails.

✏ To keep your emails organized, use labels and filters.

✏ Unsubscribe from newsletters that are not needed.

- Set email priorities according to deadlines and significance.

You may lessen email-related distractions and make sure that your inbox doesn't become a continual source of interruption by implementing these strategies.

Cooperation Instruments

To improve workflow, make use of collaborative tools like team communication apps and project management software. You can assign tasks, monitor progress, and interact with team members more effectively with the aid of these tools. You may save a lot of time by centralizing information and minimizing the need for protracted email threads.

Chapter 1: Basics of Time Management

Understanding

We must understand time management before we can implement it. We also need to understand what it isn't. If not, we won't know exactly what to do next. This raises a number of issues for a scientifically grounded process. For instance, an engineer's construction might suffer if they did not understand what gravity is.

For this reason, academic rigour is required. Furthermore, although your local college may not offer a major in time management, it does emphasize organization. Anyway, just what is this whole time management thing all about?

What Time Management Is Not

In its most basic form, time management is the discipline of setting aside specific times to do things. It is defined as "using the time that you have available in a useful and effective way" by the Cambridge Dictionary, for instance. There are easier methods. It can be viewed as the way we decide to spend our time. But I think there's more depth to it than what these definitions suggest. It entails taking our routine out of the automatic if only briefly, to make the most of our time both within and outside of the workplace. We may increase the significance of our time and memories by doing this. Please pardon my romanticism, but it's a means of adding depth to life.

But definitions are only going to take us so far. Developing a personal relationship with time management techniques is a wonderful idea. In this manner, we're engaging with it before we've even begun to count the minutes! We need to keep a few things in mind in order to accomplish this. First, time is a finite resource, but it's not a finite amount. Despite their connection, productivity and time management are not the same thing. Above all, we need to be inspired to take charge of our destiny and act proactively. We obtain direction and control by doing this.

Now, let's examine each of these hypotheses in greater depth. In doing so, I hope to gently introduce some of the principles we'll deal with throughout the book and to enhance your motivation. It can be scary to discover where our time really ends. But I encourage you to look at this as a chance. A story would be meaningless if it had neither a beginning nor an end. Would the worth of your favourite movie change if it didn't end? Would its message even remain intact? Be inspired to give your tale significance not out of dread of the end but rather out of an acceptance of its transient nature.

Science hasn't yet discovered a means to prolong a person's life indefinitely. It may be a clear challenge to overcome, but there may be more benefits than drawbacks. Temporal constraints confer value. We can also determine the activities we think are worthwhile at this moment because we are human. With a little fluctuation, we'll probably set aside eight or so hours out of a typical 24-hour day for sleeping. It's amazing to think about how many different ways the remaining 16 may be arranged! Laura, who lives next to me, paints and sculpts a lot. Then, on weekends, she will visit quaint markets, erect a small stand, and wait. Her paintings will occasionally sell like bread. And some of her pieces have stayed, even if they were present every weekend for a few weeks. She refers to them as her "pets." In the meantime, I spend much of my free time working on my goals outside of work hours while working from my home office. And we both have happy lives, even if we spend our time in quite different ways.

We are better able to comprehend the consequences of our choices when we acknowledge the finite nature of life. Dr. Laura Vanderkam, a time management specialist, discovers that viewing life in 168-hour blocks helps us understand our choices about how to use this time. She made the interesting observation that most people struggle to estimate how much time they spend on any specific task. Biases in society and the mind play a major role in this. Dr.Vanderkam, however, came up with a classy fix to assist with that. She asked a few acquaintances to write down their daily routines, and then she began analyzing the trends in their responses. She had to make a few attempts before finally hitting gold with the info she needed. Specifically, two happy people she knew managed to juggle extremely hectic lives. These people's lifestyles have not left them as worn out or depleted. This led to the following two conclusions: First, it makes a big difference to decide to allocate your time proactively to the things that are important to you. This is how the six-time mother and CEO of a seven-figure firm, Theresa Daytner, maintains equilibrium. In addition, she makes the most of that time by taking care of her business, her relationships with her family, and herself.

Time Management

OVERVIEW Action plan: Assess your existing time-management practice and establish short-term objectives.

Time management is a way of life that offers several benefits rather than just a set of techniques.

Decreased Stress: People who use efficient time management strategies experience reduced stress from work-related issues and deadline pressure.

Enhanced Productivity: By optimizing your time, you might finish more things in less time, which would give you a sense of accomplishment.

Improved Decision-Making You can make better decisions when you are more adept at managing your time because you will have a clearer idea of what matters to you.

Improved Harmony Between Work and Life: It's easier to balance job, family, and personal obligations when you manage your time well.

Essentials of Time Management

Before we go into the details of time management, let's establish a few key concepts:

Establishing Objectives: The first stage in time management is to choose your short- and long-term objectives. What goals do you have for your career and personal life?

Distinct responsibilities and goals.

Monitoring time: If you wish to get better at managing your time, you must be conscious of how you are currently spending it. Consider keeping a time journal for a week to gain more insight into your patterns.

Digital apps, calendars, and to-do lists are helpful resources for organizing your day, week, and month. Organizing your tasks is necessary to keep track of your responsibilities.

Time Wasters Have to Go: Select the time-wasting activities you do on a regular basis, such as using social media excessively or attending needless meetings. Acknowledging unhealthy patterns is the first step towards modifying them.

Commence implementing the action plan.

To help you get started on the path to effective time management, consider the following short action plan:

Self-Evaluation

You ought to record your current time usage in a time log that spans a week. Tell the truth about the habits you have.

Step 2: Set Particular Objectives

List both your short-term and long-term goals. These will direct your time management.

Sort the jobs according to priority.

To distinguish between urgent and vital tasks, utilize the Eisenhower Matrix.

Organize your week's schedule.

Organize your objectives and initiatives by using a digital planner or calendar. Don't overestimate how long an activity will take to finish.

Identify Time Wasters

Learn how to reduce or eliminate the activities that waste your time.

With this action plan, your path toward time management is far from over. We'll delve deeper into specific strategies and techniques in the upcoming chapters to help you make the most of your time and achieve your goals.

This introductory chapter provides readers with a solid foundation in time management concepts and inspires them to begin practising better time management.

Establishing Priorities and Objectives

The significance of well-defined objectives

For time management to be effective, goals must be clearly defined.

Setting and achieving goals gives your daily decisions and activities focus, direction, and a strong base.

This chapter will cover goal-setting techniques that are both relevant and practical.

SMART objectives

Using the SMART technique is a good way to set goals.

This acronym represents the five essential qualities that your objectives should have:

Particulars (Specific):

Your goals ought to be well-defined, exact, and unambiguous.

Steer clear of ambiguous goals because they can cause a lack of direction and attention.

Measurable (Measurable): Clearly define the standards by which you will measure your success.

Establish quantifiable markers that let you keep track of your goals' progress.

Realistic: Make sure that, given the circumstances, your goals are both attainable and reasonable.

When you set goals, take into account your constraints, skills, and resources.

Relevant (Relevant): Your objectives ought to be in line with your long-term vision, priorities, and values.

Verify if they have significance and relevance for you.

Time-bound: Establish precise due dates for accomplishing your objectives.

This makes the work seem more urgent and holds you responsible for finishing it.

Overview: The Significance of Effective Time Management

Time is an important resource that runs out when it's used. In order to accomplish our objectives and lead satisfying lives, we must make the most of the time we have available. Time acts as an impartial leveller for all, regardless of one's wealth, influence, or power. Everybody has the same number of hours in a day, and our lives are greatly impacted by the way we choose to use those hours.

Achieving goals both personally and professionally, keeping a positive work-life balance, and lowering stress and anxiety all depend on effective time management. We may prioritize our duties, work more productively, and complete more work in less time when we manage our time well. Additionally, it relieves the tension and annoyance that results from incomplete projects, missed deadlines, and an excessive workload.

When we don't manage our time well, we frequently find ourselves hurrying through things, making mistakes, and passing up opportunities. Burnout, decreased productivity, and even health issues may result from it. Ineffective time management can also have a detrimental effect on our relationships since it leaves us with less time to spend with friends and family or partake in enjoyable activities that advance our well-being.

But efficient time management also involves striking a balance in our lives, not merely completing more tasks.

Effective time management allows us to give our personal needs—such as rest, exercise, and self-care—priority. It assists us in living more contented and purposeful lives and prevents us from sacrificing our well-being in the name of success.

The purpose of this book is to give you useful advice on how to manage your time so that you may accomplish your goals, increase productivity, and keep a healthy work-life balance. Whether you're a student, working professional, entrepreneur, or parent staying at home, this book's concepts and approaches can help you succeed by improving your time management skills.

The best time management strategies will be covered in this book, including goal-setting, scheduling, creating work habits, increasing productivity, and striking a balance between work and personal life. We'll also talk about typical time management challenges and offer solutions.

You will have a thorough grasp of time management by the end of this book, along with the techniques and resources you need to become an expert in this crucial life skill.

Establish a Workspace

Setting up a workspace is the first step toward managing a home office. If you don't have a spare room or study, it doesn't have to be a fully functional home office. All you need is a special place to work that will resemble a workplace and help you get in the appropriate frame of mind. So, all it will take to know when it's time to start working is to go into your office. Knowing what to put in your workspace makes it easy to set up. It goes beyond simply the furnishings and apparatuses. You need to consider software, stationary, and the setup's impact on your house. Having extension cords running through busy parts of the house is a recipe for trouble, and while having a home phone may appear convenient, it may be challenging to keep track of the many expenses.

A home office needs to be carefully considered. If your house lacks a designated office space, you should pick a peaceful location where you won't be distracted. For instance, if your family spends most of their time in the dining room or living room, it is not a smart idea to set up your workplace there. Keeping things distinct will assist you in maintaining attention. A workstation is more than just a place to put your laptop and connect to the internet. Because an office plan is pre-established when we start our work, we frequently fail to recognize the amount of thought that goes into it. You'll learn from working from home that there are a number of necessities to make your life at work more convenient.

Considerations for Organizing a Workspace

I've compiled a list of necessities for a home office or workspace in this section. It is more important to emphasize the needs that will have the most influence than it is to go out and buy a ton of goods. These make up the foundation of a quality workspace.

Choosing the Proper Location

I know I mentioned this before, but let's go specific about where you should set up shop for your workstation. First of all, it's a terrific idea to use a covered balcony, study, guest room, or garage as an office. You can create the necessary divide between your living and working rooms by installing a door between these and busy areas. Because your family will be less likely to enter your office as they will know you are working, you won't become sidetracked once you enter and shut the door.

If you don't have a spare room, though, you'll need to locate a specific area where you may set up your office. In this case, you should stay away from residential locations where you know your family hangs out during the day. The sound of the kitchen blender or a television should not divert your attention. You also don't want to interfere with your family's regular schedule. It's equally annoying to have them remain silent, so you may hold an online conference as it is to have them interrupt you.

You should still arrange your workstation in a distraction-free area, even if you live alone. Windows can be a source of comfort as well as diversion. Thus, if you'd like to be close to a window, pick wisely and stay away from windows that face a busy street. Choose a location where your desk, chair, and other office supplies will fit comfortably.

Make sure you can move around a little and that you have enough plug points. The worst thing you can do is arrange your workstation so that you have to squeeze into a small, dim area. Instead of detesting your office, you should love it!

Height's Significance

The height of a working desk has an industry-standard—did you know that? Office furniture appears so uniform because of this. Desks are typically 28 to 30 inches high, making them the perfect height for people who are approximately six feet tall (Greg, 2021). But not every individual is the same height. This explains why some people struggle at their workstations while others are at ease doing so. You may adjust your desk to your preferred height and comfort level by designing your workstation. When you sit down, you should ideally be able to reach your elbows through your desk. Your screen can be set on the desk, and if your keyboard and mouse have a pull-out tray, this should be at elbow height. Additionally, you should ensure that when you sit, the tops of your thighs stay off the desk's bottom and that your feet are flat on the floor.

Ensuring your computer screen is at the proper height is another crucial component. Purchasing huge screens that are adjustable in height by placing them on a stand is a popular choice. By doing this, you can avoid hurting your neck by not glancing down at your laptop. It also keeps you from stooping over and maintains your shoulders squared.

Tips For Cooking

For single mothers, it is crucial to incorporate kitchen and cooking tricks since they make food preparation—one of the most important daily tasks—simpler.

Single mothers frequently have a lot on their plate, which leaves them with little time or energy to prepare lavish meals. Cooking is made easier with the use of kitchen tricks.

With the help of the tips in this chapter, single mothers may whip up wholesome and delectable meals fast, feeding their families well while saving money and time.

In addition to improving the general well-being of single mothers and their kids, kitchen and cooking tips help them reclaim control and balance in their lives.

1. SET UP IN BULK.

Weeknights in the homes of single mothers may rapidly turn into a frenzy of activity, especially when balancing the schedules of all the family members. It is quite helpful to prepare in bulk and shop strategically if you want to manage this hectic lifestyle.

When available space allows, think about buying greater quantities of common home supplies like paper towels. This can result in financial savings as well as ensuring that you have an adequate supply of necessities, particularly if you can take advantage of bulk discounts.

Make time this weekend to do a thorough weekly grocery shopping that includes everything you need. This enables you to stock up on necessary items, guaranteeing that your family's dinners will always have everything they need.

Make your weeknight dinners easier by prepping large, satisfying one-pot meals. Over several days, these might be a handy option for lunches and dinners.

Preparing these meals ahead of time helps you spend less time in the kitchen on hectic evenings.

Accept your slow cooker as an indispensable kitchen ally. This multipurpose tool might be very useful for working single mothers. You might even think about spending money on a smart version that lets you oversee and manage cooking from a distance. When you have to pick up your kids from their extracurricular activities or are running late for work, this tool comes in useful.

Making meals in bulk and shopping strategically can simplify everyday tasks, lessen stress, and even save money. Smart kitchen equipment and slow cookers are examples of tools that may be used to increase productivity and create a more harmonious work-life balance for parents and workers.

2. Organize a pizza night every week.

For single mothers, setting up a weekly pizza night at home can be revolutionary, with several advantages that support a better work-life balance. This special night, when the emphasis is on rest rather than cooking, is essential to enabling single mothers to spend quality time with their kids.

It offers a priceless chance for meaningful time spent together, strengthening emotional ties and creating enduring memories. It also provides a respite from the daily grind, enabling moms and children to unwind and genuinely enjoy each other's company without having to worry about cooking or going out to eat.

This recurring ritual gives the family routine a sense of stability and predictability, which is particularly consoling for homes with lone parents. It also emphasizes the significance of self-care and the worth of spending easy, enjoyable times with others.

To put it simply, setting up a weekly pizza night at home is a simple yet effective way for single mothers to make time for family time enjoyable and memorable, even with all of life's responsibilities.

3. ORDER GROCERIES ONLINE.

Purchasing groceries online is a convenient and time-saving option for single mothers who are balancing jobs, domestic tasks, and parenthood.

It makes it easier to navigate congested marketplaces with kids in tow, a sometimes difficult chore. Single mothers can purchase online from the comfort of their homes and choose from a large variety of products, saving valuable time that they can use to spend with their kids.

Because doorstep delivery reduces the need for transportation, it's also a more environmentally responsible option.

Internet grocery shopping gives single mothers the freedom to organize their schedules more effectively, feel less stressed, and spend more quality time with their kids, which makes it a vital tool in the contemporary parent's toolbox.

4. ADVANCE MEAL PREP.

One of the most important and beneficial strategies for single mothers is meal prep. First off, eliminating the need for everyday cooking frees up important time throughout the busy workday.

By enabling mothers to plan and prepare well-balanced, homemade meals ahead of time, meal prep also encourages healthier eating habits by decreasing the need for processed or fast food.

It is financially advantageous because it eliminates impulsive purchases and food waste. Meal prepping also provides peace of mind because it ensures that the family will always have wholesome meals, even on the busiest days.

Essentially, it gives single mothers the ability to manage their family's diet, schedule, and general health, which makes it a vital tool in their day-to-day lives.

Why certain tactics are more effective than others

There are many different tactics that we often encounter when attempting to improve our time management skills, all of which seem to promise positive outcomes. But not every strategy works for everyone, and depending on the circumstance and the person, some are more successful than others. That begs the question, though: why are some techniques more effective than others?

Numerous elements, both innate to the person and influenced by their surroundings, have a role in the response to this query. Below, we'll examine these variables.

Individual flexibility

Every person is different, and these differences can have an impact on how well a time management plan works for them. These may include but are not limited to, the capacity for concentration, the inclination for multitasking or single-tasking, and resistance to distraction. As a result, a tactic that suits one individual well might not be suitable for another. Therefore, a key element influencing the strategy's effectiveness is the individual's ability to adapt.

Contextual Elements

The efficiency of a strategy is also significantly influenced by the milieu in which an individual operates. The success of a strategy can be impacted by variables like the work environment, demands of the job or studies, and personal obligations. A tactic that functions well in a calm, distraction-free setting might not do as well in a busy, boisterous one.

Implementation Ease

Not every time management technique is as simple to use as the others. Some are easier and more direct, while others call for thorough planning and preparation. The success of a plan might be influenced by how simple it is to implement. Easier to comprehend and use solutions that are generally preferred by people and lead to greater success.

Flexibility in Strategy

A strategy's flexibility is its capacity to adjust to various situations. Certain techniques are quite strict and must be followed exactly, which might be difficult if something unforeseen happens or the situation changes. However, more flexible solutions allow for some degree of flexibility, which can facilitate their adoption and boost their efficacy.

Extended-Duration Efficiency

While certain tactics might yield immediate benefits, they might not be long-term viable or efficient. For instance, working continuously could boost output temporarily but eventually cause exhaustion and burnout. As a result, a strategy's long-term efficacy is a crucial consideration.

Selecting and putting into practice the best time management plan for you requires an understanding of why some tactics are more effective than others. Since every individual is different, what suits one may not suit another. As a result, it's critical to experiment with many approaches to determine which one best fits your unique requirements and situation. We'll examine some of the most well-liked and successful time management techniques in the ensuing chapters, along with practical implementation tips.

Eisenhower Matrix Hierarchy of Needs

The foundation of effective time management is prioritization, which is the process of determining which tasks or activities are most important and should be completed first. If you don't prioritize, you risk finding yourself constantly responding to urgent but unimportant matters, which can cause stress, inefficiency, and a lack of progress toward your goals.

The Eisenhower Matrix, named after a former U.S. president, is one commonly used tool for prioritizing. President Dwight D. Eisenhower is renowned for his extraordinary ability to manage his time. The matrix is a straightforward yet incredibly powerful tool for dividing jobs into four groups according to their significance and urgency.

Important and Urgent (Quadrant I): This quadrant contains critical and urgent tasks. They should be given priority and need to be attended to right away. If these assignments are not completed on time, there might be serious repercussions, including deadlines, emergencies, or crises.

Tasks in Quadrant II, "Important but Not Urgent," are crucial for achieving your long-term goals and objectives but aren't always time-sensitive. The completion of these duties, which call for planning, is essential to reaching your biggest successes. Strategic planning, skill development, and relationship building are a few examples.

Quadrant III: Urgent but Not Important: Although the tasks in this quadrant are urgent, they don't make a major impact on your long-term objectives or priorities. They are frequent disruptions or diversions that, if not handled carefully, can take up your time. To free up time for more important things, these tasks must be minimized or delegated.

Tasks in the fourth quadrant, "Not Urgent and Not Important," are not urgent nor significant. They should be cut back on or removed from your calendar because they are time wasters. This includes things like using social media excessively, aimlessly browsing the web, and attending pointless meetings.

When deciding how best to divide up your time and energy, the Eisenhower Matrix is a useful tool. It assists you in concentrating on Quadrant II, where you should ideally allocate a large amount of your time because they are the kinds of jobs that are necessary for both personal growth and long-term success. You can increase your productivity and give priority to tasks that are consistent with your values and goals by limiting

Quadrants III and IV and making the most effort to address Quadrant I.

Section Three:

PRIORITIZATION: THE ART OF EFFECTIVE DECISION-MAKING MASTERED

We have now reached a crucial phase in our quest to discover the mysteries of productivity and time management: prioritization. One of the main components of efficient time management is the capacity to prioritize duties and obligations, which is essential in determining how our daily lives unfold.

However, what precisely is the art of prioritization, and how can it assist you in recognizing and concentrating on what is most important? Let's dive deep into this essential ability, using real-world situations to inspire us as we explore methods like recognizing your "Big Rocks," the Eisenhower Matrix, and the ABCD Method.

The Skill of Setting Priorities

Determining the relative priority and urgency of tasks, activities, or goals in your life is the technique of prioritization. It involves choosing wisely where to focus your attention, effort, and financial resources. If you don't prioritize your tasks well, you run the risk of being pulled in many ways all the time and responding to the most pressing issue rather than actively working toward your objectives.

Think of your day as a vessel and your chores as different-sized stones. Everything fits snugly if you fill the jar with the largest stones (your most important chores) first, then the smaller ones (less critical jobs). But if you begin with the smaller stones, later on, the larger ones won't fit. Putting the big rocks first is the essence of priority, as this metaphor demonstrates.

Finding Your Large Rocks

The phrase "Big Rocks" refers to the idea that you should prioritize your most important duties above all else. It is taken from Stephen R. Covey's book "First Things First." The essential tasks that complement your principles, long-term ambitions, and goals are known as these "Big Rocks".

First, define your goals in order to determine your "Big Rocks." What are your career and personal objectives? What is most important to you? Once these priorities have been determined, divide them into manageable steps. These actions turn into your "Big Rocks."

If your objective is to increase your physical fitness, for example, your "Big Rocks" could include frequent health check-ups, meal planning, and daily exercise. You can devote time and effort to these important tasks by identifying them, which will help you move closer to your goals.

Self-awareness: Its Significance and Progress

The capacity to comprehend and identify one's ideas, sentiments, and emotions is known as self-awareness. It is the basis of awareness and is frequently regarded as essential to mental health.

There are various forms of self-awareness, such as emotional self-awareness, which is the recognition of one's feelings, and cognitive self-awareness, which is the ability to identify one's ideas and beliefs. There's also social self-awareness, which is the capacity to recognize how other people could interpret one's behaviours and demeanour.

Early childhood is where self-awareness growth starts, and it lasts the rest of life. It is believed to have a close relationship with the development of the prefrontal cortex, which is the part of the brain in charge of making decisions and solving problems.

Being able to reflect on one's feelings and thoughts, or to be introspective, is one of the most crucial components of self-awareness. In addition to assisting people in making better judgments, this can help people gain a better understanding of their actions and motivations. Furthermore, because self-awareness enables one to place oneself in the shoes of others, it can also aid in the development of empathy and understanding for others.

Self-awareness is not necessarily a good thing, though. For example, excessive self-awareness might result in depressive, anxious, and self-doubting feelings. Furthermore, some people could have trouble identifying their thoughts and feelings and struggle with self-awareness.

To increase their self-awareness, people might employ a variety of techniques. Mindfulness meditation is one of the best; it entails paying attention to one's thoughts and feelings without passing judgment. Exercises in self-reflection, counselling, and journaling can also be beneficial.

In summary, self-awareness is a multifaceted and intricate idea that is essential to mental health. It is the capacity to comprehend and identify one's ideas, sentiments, and emotions, and it is intimately related to prefrontal brain development. In terms of self-awareness, it's critical to find a balance because too much of it can be harmful and too little can impede personal development. With the correct resources, people can become more self-aware and lead happier lives.

There once was a young prince named Alexander who lived in a distant realm. Raised in the height of luxury, he was the only child of the king and queen. He had riches, power, and status—everything he could ask for. But Alexander was not content in spite of all of this. He sensed that something was lacking in his life, but he was unable to identify what it was.

The prince decided to take a mental health walk in the forest one day. He discovered an elderly hermit living in a tiny home tucked away in the woods as he strolled by. Alexander had heard tales about the wise hermit's guidance benefiting a great number of people in the realm. He, therefore, decided to consult the hermit.

The prince was invited by the hermit inside his cabin, where he listened intently as Alexander opened up to him. "I have everything I could ever want," the king replied, "but I still feel unfulfilled. I don't know what's missing in my life, but I can't shake the feeling that something is not right."

The hermit cast a compassionate and wise glance at the prince. "Your problem, my dear prince," he said, "is that you lack self-awareness. You have not yet learned to understand and recognize your thoughts, feelings, and emotions.

Without this understanding, you will never truly be happy."

Prince was taken aback. It never occurred to him to think of it that way. The hermit continued by explaining that self-awareness is the cornerstone of consciousness and that maintaining mental health depends on it. Additionally, he mentioned that there are various types of self-awareness, including social, emotional, and cognitive types. He also discusses the value of introspection, or the capacity to consider one's feelings and ideas.

The hermit then gave the prince a mission. He instructed the prince to return to the cabin in a week and to dedicate some time each day to introspection and self-reflection. In addition, he was to spend some time in nature, paying attention to his thoughts and emotions as they emerged.

Following the instructions, the prince gained a deeper understanding of himself than he had ever had in a week. He realized that he had never really taken the time to understand his own needs and desires and had instead been living his life in accordance with the expectations of others.

A week later, the prince returned to the hermit's cottage a different person. He experienced a level of contentment and serenity that he had never experienced before. He expressed gratitude to the hermit for his insight and vowed to spend the rest of his life pursuing self-awareness.

The prince lived a life filled with meaning and purpose after that day. His inner voice now guided him instead of the demands of others. Additionally, he was more understanding, kind, and empathetic toward others around him. Thus, the prince attained genuine contentment and led a happy life for the rest of his days.

Prince Alexander's self-awareness journey serves as a reminder that genuine happiness originates from the inside, not from things outside of oneself. We must take the time to comprehend and identify our ideas, sentiments, and emotions. We can only genuinely have important and fulfilling lives by doing this.

An additional crucial component of discipline is self-care. To reach our objectives, we must look after our mental, emotional, and physical health. This includes obtaining adequate rest, maintaining a nutritious diet, and engaging in stress-relieving exercises like yoga or meditation. By looking after ourselves, we can enhance our general health and keep up the drive and vitality required to accomplish our objectives.

www.ingramcontent.com/pod-product-compliance
Lightning Source LLC
Chambersburg PA
CBHW052131110526
44591CB00012B/1675